Pingu's Bouncy Fun

Pingu was having fun bouncing on his bed.

But he was making plates
jump off the kitchen shelves.

He wasn't pleased when Mother told him to stop.

He wanted to keep bouncing.

Mother told him to stay in the living room with Pinga.

But when Pingu
sat in the armchair,
he found it was
really quite bouncy.

Mother heard a noise and came back in to tell him to stop.

Chairs were not for bouncing on, she said.

Pingu got off the chair...

...and bounced on Pinga's rabbit instead.

When Father came home,
Mother was glad to take
Pinga to the shops.

Pingu asked Father to help him make something he could bounce on.

They started to collect some useful things.
The watering can wasn't one of them!

Gradually, a frame was starting to take shape.

Father tied on some canvas
and the trampoline
was finished.

**Pingu couldn't wait to try it out.
He hopped on...**

...and bounced right off onto the floor.

Pingu tried again.
This time
he bounced...

...right into Father's arms. Father said he needed more practice.

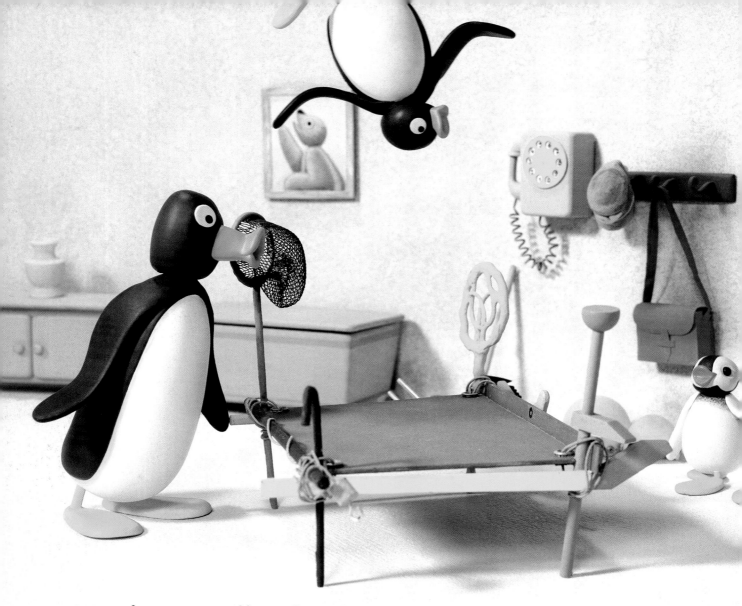

Mother walked in and wanted to know what they were doing.

Pingu somersaulted off the trampoline...

...and landed upside down, in the armchair.

Father suggested they drag the trampoline outside to play.

Mother gave them each a crash helmet, to make sure they were safe.

It was time to BOUNCE!